Book of Divine Devotions

LeShawn Fernandez

Book of Divine Devotions

LeShawn Fernandez

ARPress
ILLUMINATING IDEAS,
EMPOWERING VOICES

ARPress
45 Dan Road Suite 15
Canton MA 02021

Hotline:	1(888) 821-0229
Fax:	1(508) 545-7580

Ordering Information:
Quantity sales. Special discounts are available on quantity purchases by corporations, associations, and others. For details, contact the publisher at the address above.

Printed in the United States of America.

ISBN-13:	Softcover	979-8-89676-663-6
	eBook	979-8-89676-664-3

Library of Congress Control Number: 2026903666

Table of Contents

Introduction

I impress preachers, scholars, or the perfect church folks. I wrote didn't write this devotional to be fancy. I didn't write it to this for the warriors. For the ones carrying scars under their Sunday clothes. For the ones who have cried in silence, wondering if God still hears them. For the ones who have been through hell and somehow got up the next morning anyway.

Life has knocked me down more times than I can count. I've faced betrayal in places where I should've been covered, rejection from the very ones I thought would ride with me, and storms that left me breathless. But here's the truth: God met me in every valley. His presence showed up in my weakest moments, and His Word carried me when nothing else could.

This devotional is 39 days of raw truth, scripture, and encouragement. It's not about being perfect—it's about being real with God and letting Him heal the broken places. Each day is short on purpose—so you can pause, reflect, and let the Spirit minister to you, whether you're on your lunch break, in your car, or just trying to breathe through another long night.

While I may not know your exact struggle, I do know this: God has not forgotten you. These words are proof that you're still on His heart. My prayer is that through these pages, you'll feel seen, loved, and strengthened to keep walking—one day at a time.

Let's walk this journey together.

— LeShawn

ACKNOWLEDGMENT

First and foremost, I give honor to my Heavenly Father. Without His presence, His grace, and His unconditional love, none of this would be possible. Every word I write, every testimony I share, is a reflection of His hand on my life. I am deeply grateful for the way He has carried me through storms and reminded me that even in my weakest moments, His strength is made perfect.

This devotional is not just my work—it is His work through me, and to Him be all the glory.

DEDICATION

I dedicate this book to my soul tribe—the kings and queens who are walking this healing journey right alongside me. It hasn't been easy, but together we have chosen growth over bitterness, love over fear, and healing over hiding.

You remind me daily that transformation is possible when we lean on God and on each other. I am forever grateful to God for placing you in my life. Your courage, your prayers, and your willingness to keep pressing forward inspire me more than you know.

May this devotional serve as a reminder that we are never walking alone—God is with us, and we are with each other.

AUTHOR'S NOTE

When I look back over my life, I see chapter after chapter where God's hand carried me, even when I didn't understand what He was doing. Writing this devotional has been more than just a project—it's been a mirror of my own healing journey. Every prayer, every reflection, and every declaration has come out of real moments where I had to trust God more than I trusted my own strength.

This devotional is not about perfection—it's about progress. It's about choosing healing when brokenness felt easier. It's about surrendering when holding on felt safer. And most of all, it's about reminding you that God is faithful, no matter what storm you're facing.

I pray that as you walk through these pages, you don't just read my words—you hear His. I pray you feel less alone, more seen, and more equipped to keep moving forward. Healing isn't always pretty, but it's always worth it. And I believe, with all my heart, that if God did it for me, He will do it for you too.

With love and faith,

LeShawn Fernandez

Day 1
WHY SURRENDER?

Title: Surrender: Laying It All at the Cross

AFFIRMATION:

Today, I choose to stop wrestling with God and start resting in Him.

SCRIPTURE:

> "And we know that in all things God works for the
> good of those who love Him, who have been called
> according to His purpose." — **ROMANS 8:28 (NIV)**

STORY:

I know what it feels like to hold on so tight that your hands start to hurt—trying to control outcomes, protect your heart, and fix everything yourself. I tried to "manage" my pain after church hurt, and all it did was exhaust me. But the moment I surrendered—when I finally said, "God, this belongs to You"—He began working in ways I couldn't see, in rooms I didn't even know existed.

REFLECTION:

What are you carrying right now that you were never meant to? Write it down, and pray over it today, asking God to take it.

____

____

____

____

____

DECLARATION:

I release control. God is working this out for my good, even if I can't see it yet.

PRAYER:

Father, I lay my burdens at Your feet today. I trust that every detail of my life is in Your hands. Show me how to rest in Your will. Amen.

TO THE ONE WHO FEELS FORGOTTEN

Title: God Sees You

AFFIRMATION:
My name is still written on God's heart.

SCRIPTURE:
> "So do not fear, for I am with you; do not be dismayed, for I am your God. I will strengthen you and help you; I will uphold you with my righteous right hand." — **ISAIAH 41:10 (NIV)**

STORY:
There was a season when I felt invisible—ignored by people who once called me family in the faith. I thought God had turned His face from me too. But the truth? God was closer than ever, holding me steady when my trust in people collapsed.

The enemy wants you to confuse people's failure with God's character. Don't. People may walk away, but God never has and never will.

REFLECTION:
Where have you confused human failure with God's love?

DECLARATION:
Even in my loneliness, God is present. I am not abandoned.

PRAYER:
Lord, thank You for seeing me when I feel unseen. Remind me that Your presence is constant, and that my name is always on Your heart. Amen.

Day 3

LOVE THAT
WON'T LET GO

Title: The Unshakable Love of God

AFFIRMATION:

Nothing I've done can separate me from His love.

SCRIPTURE:

> "For God so loved the world that He gave His one
> and only Son, that whoever believes in Him shall not
> perish but have eternal life." — **JOHN 3:16 (NIV)**

STORY:

There were days I didn't even love myself, let alone feel worthy of God's love. Shame from hurt and disappointment had me questioning everything. But His love? It doesn't let go. It's not fragile. It doesn't walk away when you're at your lowest.

God's love is a warrior—it fights for you when you can't fight for yourself.

REFLECTION:

When was the last time you let yourself believe that you are truly loved by God?

____

____

____

____

____

DECLARATION:

God's love is my anchor and my covering; I will not doubt it today.

PRAYER:

Father, thank You for loving me in ways I can't comprehend. Teach me to receive Your love without conditions. Amen.

Day 4
THE FIRST STEP BACK

Title: Coming Home to God

AFFIRMATION:
It's never too late to return.

SCRIPTURE:
> "But while he was still a long way off, his father saw
> him and was filled with compassion for him…"
> — LUKE 15:20 (NIV)

STORY:
I remember the first time I decided to walk back toward God after my hurt. I was scared—What if He was angry? What if He rejected me like they did?

But instead of punishment, I found open arms. God's welcome is always full of compassion, not condemnation. You don't have to fix yourself first—you just have to take the first step back.

REFLECTION:

What's one small way you can take a step toward God today?

____

____

____

____

____

____

DECLARATION:

I am returning to God's presence, and His arms are open wide.

PRAYER:

Lord, meet me on my way back to You. Give me courage to step toward Your love again. Amen.

Day 5

ONCE YOU
RETURN HOME

Title: Once You Return Home to God

AFFIRMATION:
God welcomes me home like the father welcomed the prodigal son—with unconditional love and forgiveness.

SCRIPTURE:

> "But the father said to his servants, 'Quick! Bring the
> best robe and put it on him. Put a ring on his finger
> and sandals on his feet. Bring the fattened calf and
> kill it. Let's have a feast and celebrate. For this son of
> mine was dead and is alive again; he was lost and is
> found.' So they began to celebrate."
> **— LUKE 15:22–24 (NIV)**

STORY:
Jesus told the parable of the prodigal son to show us God's unconditional love and forgiveness for those who repent, even after

turning away from Him. The father didn't shame his son when he came home—he celebrated him. That's the same way God welcomes us: arms open, love unshaken, ready to restore what was broken.

REFLECTION:
How does it feel knowing that God welcomes you back with open arms, forgiving you completely, no matter what your past looked like?

____

____

____

____

____

____

DECLARATION:
God rejoices over me when I return. His love covers my mistakes, and His forgiveness makes me new.

PRAYER:
Lord, thank You for welcoming me back with open arms, for forgiving me of my past, and for allowing me to start brand new in our relationship. Amen.

Day 6
NOW THAT YOU ARE HOME

Title: Now That You Are Back in God's Grace

AFFIRMATION:
God's grace sustains me daily.

SCRIPTURE:
> "For it is by grace you have been saved, through
> faith—and this is not from yourselves, it is the gift of
> God—not by works, so that no one can boast."
> **— EPHESIANS 2:8–9 (NIV)**

STORY:
Grace is God's unlimited favor and love—it's a gift we don't deserve and can't earn. I used to think I had to prove myself worthy of God's love, as if my performance determined His acceptance. But the Word reminds us that salvation is not about what we do—it's about what Jesus already did.

When you return home to God, grace is what keeps you. Grace lifts the weight of striving and whispers: You're already loved. You're already chosen.

REFLECTION:

How do you feel knowing that grace is God's unlimited favor and love—given freely, not earned?

____

____

____

____

____

____

DECLARATION:

"For sin shall no longer be your master, because you
are not under the law, but under grace."
— ROMANS 6:14 (NIV)

I live in freedom because of His grace.

PRAYER:

Lord, thank You for Your grace that frees me from sin's grip. Thank You for giving me unconditional love and favor. Help me to walk boldly in the gift of grace every day. Amen.

Day 7

WALKING IN FORGIVENESS

Title: The Power of Forgiveness

AFFIRMATION:

Because I am forgiven, I can forgive.

SCRIPTURE:

> "Be kind and compassionate to one another, forgiving
> each other, just as in Christ God forgave you."
> — **EPHESIANS 4:32 (NIV)**

STORY:

Forgiveness used to feel impossible for me. The hurt cut so deep, and I thought holding onto anger protected me. But the truth? Bitterness only chained me to the pain. The moment I surrendered it to God and chose to forgive—not because they deserved it, but because I was forgiven first—I felt freedom.

Forgiveness doesn't excuse what was done. It doesn't erase the pain. But it does release you from carrying the weight. Walking in forgiveness is walking in the freedom God already purchased for you.

REFLECTION:
Who is God asking you to release through forgiveness today? What weight are you still carrying that He wants you to lay down?

____

____

____

____

____

DECLARATION:
I choose forgiveness. I will not stay chained to anger. I release and walk in freedom.

PRAYER:
Father, thank You for forgiving me fully and freely. Help me extend that same grace to others. Give me strength to let go of bitterness and walk in the freedom of forgiveness. Amen.

Day 8
STRENGTH IN THE STRUGGLE

Title: God Is My Strength

AFFIRMATION:

When I am weak, He is strong in me.

SCRIPTURE:

> "But he said to me, 'My grace is sufficient for you, for
> my power is made perfect in weakness.' Therefore I
> will boast all the more gladly about my weaknesses,
> so that Christ's power may rest on me."
> **— 2 CORINTHIANS 12:9 (NIV)**

STORY:

There were days I wanted to quit—quit ministry, quit relationships, quit fighting for my own life. The struggle was so heavy that I thought weakness meant failure. But God flipped the script. He reminded me that weakness is not the end; it's the doorway for His strength to show up.

When I stopped pretending to be strong on my own and admitted my weakness before Him, His power carried me through. What looked like breaking was really building.

REFLECTION:
Where in your life do you need to let God's strength replace your weakness?

____

____

____

____

____

____

DECLARATION:
I will not be ashamed of my weakness. God's strength is made perfect in me.

PRAYER:
Lord, thank You that I don't have to carry it all alone. In my weakness, Your strength is revealed. Teach me to lean on Your power every single day. Amen.

Day 9

PEACE IN THE CHAOS

Title: God Is My Peace

AFFIRMATION:
Even in the storm, I can rest because His peace is with me.

SCRIPTURE:
"And the peace of God, which transcends all understanding, will guard your hearts and your minds in Christ Jesus." — **PHILIPPIANS 4:7 (NIV)**

STORY:
Life doesn't always slow down just because we need it to. I've had moments where everything hit at once—family stress, health struggles, financial burdens, and spiritual battles. My mind ran in circles, and sleep wouldn't come. But in the middle of my chaos, I heard God whisper: "Be still. I am here."

Peace isn't the absence of problems—it's the presence of God in the middle of them. His peace guards your heart when fear tries to take over, and it steadies your mind when worry comes knocking.

REFLECTION:

What chaos are you facing right now? How can you invite God's peace to cover it today?

DECLARATION:

The peace of God rules over my mind and heart. Fear has no place here.

PRAYER:

Father, thank You for peace that doesn't make sense to the world but anchors me in You. Guard my heart and mind today, and help me to stay still in Your presence. Amen.

Day 10
JOY THAT STAYS

Title: Finding Joy Again

AFFIRMATION:

My joy is not fragile—it's rooted in the Lord.

SCRIPTURE:

> "The joy of the Lord is your strength."
> **— NEHEMIAH 8:10 (NIV)**

STORY:

Happiness comes and goes, but joy is different. There was a time when I thought I lost my joy for good. Disappointment had drained me, and grief had silenced my laughter. But slowly, God began to remind me that His joy isn't tied to circumstances—it's anchored in who He is.

The joy of the Lord is steady, even when life feels unstable. It's the kind of joy that can rise up in tears, whisper hope in dark seasons, and give strength when everything else feels weak.

REFLECTION:

Where have you mistaken happiness for joy? How can you lean on the joy of the Lord today instead of waiting for circumstances to change?

____

____

____

____

____

____

DECLARATION:

The joy of the Lord is my strength. I will not let life steal what God has planted in me.

PRAYER:

Lord, thank You that my joy is not fragile, but rooted in You. Restore my laughter, renew my strength, and let my life reflect Your joy no matter the season. Amen.

Day 11

WAITING WITHOUT WASTING

Title: Purpose in the Waiting

AFFIRMATION:

My waiting season is not wasted—God is working while I wait.

SCRIPTURE:

> "But they that wait upon the Lord shall renew their
> strength; they shall mount up with wings as eagles;
> they shall run, and not be weary; and they shall walk,
> and not faint." — **ISAIAH 40:31 (KJV)**

STORY:

Waiting is one of the hardest parts of walking with God. I used to think waiting meant God had forgotten me or that my prayers didn't matter. But over time, I learned that waiting isn't punishment—it's preparation.

God strengthens us in the waiting. He stretches our faith, builds endurance, and teaches us to trust His timing instead of forcing our own. What feels like a delay is often God positioning things in ways we couldn't see.

REFLECTION:

Where in your life are you waiting right now? How can you shift your perspective from frustration to preparation?

____

____

____

____

____

____

DECLARATION:

My waiting season is not wasted. God is renewing my strength and preparing me for what's ahead.

PRAYER:

Lord, thank You for being faithful even in the waiting. Teach me to trust Your timing and to find strength in You while I wait. Amen.

Day 12

WHEN FEAR TRIES TO WIN

Title: Faith Over Fear

AFFIRMATION:
Fear will not control me—my faith is bigger.

SCRIPTURE:
> "For God has not given us a spirit of fear, but of power
> and of love and of a sound mind."
> — **2 TIMOTHY 1:7 (NKJV)**

STORY:
Fear used to run my life. Fear of failure. Fear of rejection. Fear that God wouldn't come through for me. The enemy knows that fear paralyzes—it keeps us stuck in what-ifs instead of moving in God's promises.

But the Word reminds me: fear is not from God. What He gave me is power, love, and a sound mind. Every time fear rises up, I have to answer it with faith. Faith shifts the atmosphere. Faith pushes back the lies.

REFLECTION:

What fear has been holding you back lately? How can you speak faith over it today?

____

____

____

____

____

____

DECLARATION:

I will not live in fear. I walk in the power, love, and sound mind that God has given me.

PRAYER:

Father, thank You for replacing my fear with faith. Strengthen me to trust You when fear whispers lies. Help me walk boldly in the power of Your Spirit. Amen.

Day 13
HEALING TAKES TIME

Title: God Heals in Layers

AFFIRMATION:
I give myself permission to heal at God's pace.

SCRIPTURE:
> "He heals the brokenhearted and binds up their
> wounds." — **PSALM 147:3 (NIV)**

STORY:
I used to think healing meant snapping my fingers and never feeling the pain again. But real healing? It's a process. Sometimes God heals instantly, but more often He heals us in layers—peeling back the hurt little by little, teaching us to lean on Him in the process.

Healing isn't about pretending you're fine. It's about allowing God to touch the broken places, even when it's uncomfortable. Every layer He heals makes you stronger, softer, and more dependent on His love.

REFLECTION:

What wound in your heart still needs God's healing touch? Have you been rushing the process instead of letting Him work in layers?

____

____

____

____

____

DECLARATION:

I will not rush my healing. God is binding up my wounds day by day.

PRAYER:

Lord, thank You for being patient with me in my healing journey. Heal me layer by layer until my brokenness becomes a testimony of Your grace. Amen.

Day 14
WHEN THE PAST KNOCKS

Title: I Am Not Who I Used to Be

AFFIRMATION:
My past does not define me—God does.

SCRIPTURE:
> "Therefore, if anyone is in Christ, the new creation has
> come: The old has gone, the new is here!"
> **— 2 CORINTHIANS 5:17 (NIV)**

STORY:
The enemy loves to remind us of who we used to be. Old mistakes, bad decisions, shameful memories—they come knocking at the door of your mind, trying to convince you nothing has changed. I've been there, replaying moments I wish I could erase.

But here's the truth: when Christ makes you new, the old has no authority over you anymore. You don't have to live chained to yesterday. You are not your past. You are redeemed, restored, and brand new in Him.

REFLECTION:
What "old self" are you still letting define your identity? How can you walk boldly in your new life in Christ today?

____

____

____

____

____

____

DECLARATION:
The old me is gone. I am a new creation in Christ, and I will not go back.

PRAYER:
Father, thank You for making me new. Silence the lies of my past and help me live boldly as the person You've called me to be. Amen.

Day 15

GOD'S WORD
STILL STANDS

Title: Standing on His Promises

AFFIRMATION:

Every promise God made over my life is still true.

SCRIPTURE:

> "The grass withers and the flowers fall, but the word
> of our God endures forever." — **ISAIAH 40:8 (NIV)**

STORY:

There were moments when I doubted if God's promises still applied to me. Life had hit me so hard that I started to wonder if maybe His Word had an expiration date. But every time I opened my Bible, I was reminded—His promises do not expire. His Word is alive, unshakable, and still standing when everything else falls apart.

People may change their mind. Circumstances may shift. But God's Word? It remains. If He said it, He will do it.

REFLECTION:
What promise from God do you need to stand on again today, even if your circumstances haven't changed yet?

____

____

____

____

____

DECLARATION:
God's Word is my foundation. What He spoke over my life will come to pass.

PRAYER:
Lord, thank You that Your Word never fails. Strengthen me to stand on Your promises no matter what I see around me. Amen.

Day 16
LOOK AT GOD THROUGH THE STORM

Title: Seeing God in the Rain

AFFIRMATION:
Even when I'm standing in the storm, I can still see God's hand at work.

SCRIPTURE:
> "When you pass through the waters, I will be with you..." — ISAIAH 43:2 (NIV)

STORY:
There have been seasons where the storm didn't let up, and I wondered if I would drown. But in the middle of the downpour, I learned that God doesn't disappear—He shows up. The storm sharpened my vision. Instead of focusing on the rain, I lifted my eyes and said, "Look at God."

Storms don't hide Him. They reveal Him.

REFLECTION:

What storm are you facing right now? Can you shift your focus from the rain to the One who holds you steady?

____

____

____

____

____

DECLARATION:

In the storm, I will not panic—I will look at God, knowing He is working all things together for my good.

PRAYER:

Father, thank You for being present in my storms. Teach me to keep my eyes on You instead of the waves. Amen.

Day 17
BREAKING THE CHAINS

Title: Breaking Generational Curses

AFFIRMATION:

I am not bound by my family's past—I am free in Christ.

SCRIPTURE:

> "He brought them out of darkness, the utter darkness,
> and broke away their chains." — **PSALM 107:14 (NIV)**

STORY:

For years, I felt trapped by patterns that seemed to run through my family—hurt, fear, shame. But God reminded me that curses don't have the final word—Christ does. Every time I declare freedom over my life and my bloodline, the chains lose power.

I am walking in a healed legacy. What broke others will not break me.

REFLECTION:

What pattern in your life is God calling you to break today?

____

____

____

____

____

____

DECLARATION:

I choose healing over history. The chains of the past have no power over me.

PRAYER:

Lord, thank You for breaking every chain. Teach me to walk boldly in freedom and to create a healed legacy. Amen.

Day 18

FROM MENTAL ANGUISH TO RESILIENCE

Title: The Warrior Who Broke Free

AFFIRMATION:
My mind is not a prison—I am free and renewed in Christ.

SCRIPTURE:
> "My grace is sufficient for you, for my power is made perfect in weakness." — **2 CORINTHIANS 12:9 (NIV)**

STORY:
I know what it feels like to battle in the mind, to fight thoughts that scream louder than truth. For a long time, I carried that anguish in silence. But the moment I laid it bare before God, He turned my pain into power. Speaking my struggle didn't make me weak—it made me free.

What once weighed me down is now the very place God shows His strength.

REFLECTION:

What silent battle are you carrying? How would it feel to let God meet you in that place?

____

____

____

____

____

____

DECLARATION

My anguish is not my identity. I am a warrior, and God is turning my weakness into strength.

PRAYER:

Father, thank You for renewing my mind daily. Silence the lies of the enemy and remind me that I am free. Amen.

Day 19
FAITH, THERAPY, ACCOUNTABILITY

Title: Strength in Vulnerability

AFFIRMATION:

I honor God when I admit I need help and lean into healing.

SCRIPTURE:

> "Carry each other's burdens, and in this way you will
> fulfill the law of Christ." — **GALATIANS 6:2 (NIV)**

STORY:

There was a time I thought I had to carry everything alone. Faith told me to pray, but pride told me to hide. I learned that God doesn't call us to hide—He calls us to heal. And sometimes healing means prayer, therapy, and trusted accountability all working together.

It's not weakness to reach for help. It's wisdom.

REFLECTION:

What burden are you carrying alone that God may be asking you to share with someone trustworthy?

____

____

____

____

____

____

DECLARATION:

I choose faith and healing. I am not ashamed of my journey—I am strengthened through it.

PRAYER:

Lord, thank You for placing the right people and resources in my life. Give me courage to use them as You guide me toward healing. Amen.

Day 20

WARRIOR
WITH PURPOSE

Title: My Story Has Power

AFFIRMATION:

What was meant to break me is now the foundation of my purpose.

SCRIPTURE:

> "They overcame him by the blood of the Lamb and by
> the word of their testimony..."
> **— REVELATION 12:11 (NIV)**

STORY:

I used to think my story disqualified me, but I've learned it's my story that makes me powerful. The same scars I wanted to hide became proof of God's healing hand. Every tear, every battle, every valley—it all points to His faithfulness.

My testimony isn't shame. It's strength. It's the reminder that God can take what was meant for harm and use it for good.

REFLECTION:

What part of your story have you kept hidden? What would it look like to let God use it as a testimony?

____

____

____

____

____

DECLARATION:

I am a warrior. My scars are not my shame—they are proof of God's glory in my life.

PRAYER:

Father, thank You for turning my pain into purpose. Use my story to bring healing to others and glory to Your name. Amen.

Day 21
Breath When The Walls Close In

Title: Finding God When Panic Rises

AFFIRMATION:
Even when panic tries to steal my peace, God breathes calm into me.

SCRIPTURE:
> "You will keep in perfect peace those whose minds
> are steadfast, because they trust in you."
> — ISAIAH 26:3 (NIV)

STORY:
There were moments when I felt the walls closing in—anxiety tightening around my chest. Fear whispered that I couldn't handle it. But I learned to pause, breathe, and breathe again. In the silence of prayer, God whispered back: "I've got you." His peace didn't depend on my circumstances—it depended on His presence.

REFLECTION:

When panic rises, what small breath can you give to God today?

____

____

____

____

____

DECLARATION:

I will lean into God's peace. My breath is an act of worship and surrender to His calming presence.

PRAYER:

Father, thank You for breathing peace into my panic. Help me to anchor in You when fear tries to overwhelm. Amen.

Day 22

HEALING WORDS, HEALING HEART

TITLE: The Power of Speaking Truth

AFFIRMATION:

What I speak shapes my soul—today I choose truth.

SCRIPTURE:

> "The tongue has the power of life and death..."
> — **PROVERBS 18:21 (NIV)**

STORY:

My mind can be a battlefield of lies—from shame, doubt, or regret. But I discovered that speaking God's truth over myself is like medicine for the soul. "You are seen. You are worthy. You are healing." I've seen how a single sentence of truth can counteract years of negative whispering.

REFLECTIOM:

What lie has your mind believed for too long? What truth can you speak over yourself today?

____

____

____

____

____

DECLARATION:

I will speak life today. My words will mirror God's love, not the enemy's lies.

PRAYER:

Lord, help me to guard my words and to pour Your truth over my heart daily. Amen.

Day 23

COMMUNITY AS HIS CURE

Title: We Heal Together

AFFIRMATION:
I am not meant to walk this journey alone—God placed community around me for healing.

SCRIPTURE:
"Therefore encourage one another and build each other up..." — 1 THESSALONIANS 5:11 (NIV)

STORY:
I used to think asking for help was weakness—but true healing came when I let my walls down. I shared my pain with trusted friends, and their prayers became my oxygen. Their encouragement whispered: "You are not alone." Healing wasn't a solo mission—it was a shared journey.

REFLECTION:

Who can you invite into your struggle today, someone who will speak life and grace over you?

DECLARATION:

I will lean into community. God's promised presence often comes through others.

PRAYER:

Father, thank You for the people You've placed in my life. Help me to receive and to lean in when I'm weary. Amen.

FIGHTING FEAR WITH FAITH

Title: Faith That Moves

AFFIRMATION:
When fear tries to paralyze me, I'll take one step forward in faith.

SCRIPTURE:
> "Be strong and courageous. Do not be afraid... for the
> Lord your God goes with you." — **JOSHUA 1:9 (NIV)**

STORY:
Fear's tactic is to keep us stuck. But God whispers, "Move forward."
Even a small step—picking up your Bible again, reaching out for
help, praying when all you feel is numb—pushes the darkness back.
Every step in faith is a refusal to live in fear.

REFLECTION:

What small step of faith can you take today, even if your fear is still right there?

____

____

____

____

____

____

DECLARATION:

I choose faith over fear. I will move forward, trusting that God is with me.

PRAYER:

Lord, strengthen my faith when fear rises. Help me to trust You one step at a time. Amen.

Day 25
SCARS TELL STORIES

Title: Beautiful Scars

AFFIRMATION:
My scars are not shame—they are stories of survival and God's grace.

SCRIPTURE:
> "We also rejoice in our sufferings… because suffering produces perseverance; perseverance, character; and character, hope." — **ROMANS 5:3–4 (NIV)**

STORY:
I've carried wounds long enough to think they were shameful. But now I see—those scars are proof that I survived. They've shaped my character, built my faith, and made me who I am. They aren't marks of defeat—they're crown points of victory told through grace.

REFLECTION:

How can you begin to view your scars as badges of survival rather than shame?

____

____

____

____

____

____

DECLARATION:

My scars tell a story of God's faithfulness. I walk in their testimony, not their pain.

PRAYER:

Father, thank You for redeeming my scars. Let them remind me—and others—that Your grace transforms brokenness into beauty. Amen.

Day 26

MY WARRIOR STORY

Title: Writing My Story to Heal

AFFIRMATION:

My life story is a lifeline—for me and others.

SCRIPTURE:

> "We overcome by the blood of the Lamb and through
> the word of our testimony..."
> — **REVELATION 12:11 (NIV)**

STORY:

I've walked through places so dark that silence felt safer than speaking. But as I pressed into my story—releasing the shame, unpacking the wounds—God turned it into a map of hope. "The Story of a Warrior" isn't just words on a page—it's a lifeline. If my brokenness can become someone's breakthrough, then every painful chapter wasn't wasted.

REFLECTION:

What part of your story feels too raw to tell—but might heal someone else?

____

____

____

____

____

DECLARATION:

My story speaks life. My vulnerability points others to God's victory.

PRAYER:

Father, give me the courage to speak my story and to receive healing through it. Use my past to bring light into someone's darkest place. Amen.

Day 27

MIRACLE IN THE RAIN

Title: When the Impossible Happens

AFFIRMATION:

What they called impossible, God calls miraculous.

SCRIPTURE:

> "With man this is impossible, but with God all things
> are possible." — **MATTHEW 19:26 (NIV)**

STORY:

Doctors said she had no chance. My body was injured, my health fragile, and I was high-risk. But God said, "Miracle." She weighed one pound nine ounces, fragile and weak—and yet she spoke, ran, learned, excelled. If God can bring life out of that, He can bring breakthrough to my next impossible season.

REFLECTION:

What situation around you seems too far gone to be restored?

____

____

____

____

____

____

DECLARATION:

God is a miracle-worker. I trust Him to do what only He can in my life.

PRAYER:

Lord, I believe in Your mighty works. Help me to trust even when I can't see it, knowing that my Miracle is possible through You. Amen.

Day 28

LOOK AT GOD
IN YOUR STORM

Title: Eyes Lifted, Not Underwater

AFFIRMATION:

My storm isn't the end—He is.

SCRIPTURE:

> "Look to the Lord and His strength; seek His face
> always." — **1 CHRONICLES 16:11 (NIV)**

STORY:

The rain was relentless—and talking about it didn't change how hard it fell. But when I shifted from "Why, God?" to "Look at God!", everything changed. The storm didn't disappear—but His presence did. That chapter in Through the Rain isn't just a title—it's an invitation to stop staring down and lift your gaze toward the Giver of life.

REFLECTION:

Are you staring at your storm—or remembering the One who silences its roar?

DECLARATION:

I will look at God, not the storm. His presence steadies me.

PRAYER:

Father, lift my gaze above the wind and waves. Help me to see You as the anchor in every storm. Amen.

Day 29

BLESSED ON THE OTHER SIDE

Title: The Blessing After the Breakthrough

AFFIRMATION:

I refuse to stop at the storm—I walk toward the blessing.

SCRIPTURE:

> "Weeping may stay for the night, but rejoicing comes in the morning." — **PSALM 30:5 (NIV)**

STORY:

There were seasons when every door slammed shut, and I believed that might be it. But I learned: God doesn't leave us stuck. Breakthrough waits right after the storm rains itself out. "Don't give up," I say, "your blessing is on the other side." That's not just hope—that's a promise born from my healing journey.

REFLECTION:

Where do you need to hold on just a little longer so you can step into your blessing?

____

____

____

____

____

____

DECLARATION:

My blessing is on the way. I will not quit my breakthrough.

PRAYER:

Lord, help me to breathe through the pain and lean into hope. Let the joy that outlasts the night be mine today. Amen.

Day 30

CREATION MADE BETTER

Title: Masterpiece in Progress

AFFIRMATION:

God doesn't just fix—I am becoming more beautiful than I began.

SCRIPTURE:

"He makes every masterpiece better than the
original." **(ADAPTED FROM ISAIAH 64:8)**

STORY:

My past was broken, but God didn't just repair it—He turned it into purpose. Just like the storms sharpened my faith, my healing journey shaped me into a stronger, more compassionate warrior. I am God's masterpiece—in progress, yes, but undeniably His.

REFLECTION:

How can you see yourself as more than healed—but refined and redesigned by love?

DECLARATION:

I am God's masterpiece built through trials, shaped by grace.

PRAYER:

Father, thank You for taking what was broken and making it beautiful. Help me to walk fully accepted in my restored identity. Amen.

Closing Word
You Are a Warrior

You made it through 30 days of this devotional—but let me tell you, this is just the beginning. These past weeks were not about perfection, but about positioning. Each day you've laid something down, picked something up, and walked closer with God. That's the rhythm of a warrior: not that life is easy, but that faith stays steady.

Storms will still come. Doubts may still whisper. But the truth remains: you are not who you were on Day 1. You are stronger. You are steadier. And you are walking in the grace, peace, and power of God.

Never forget—your story is not your shame, it's your strength. The very thing the enemy thought would break you is now proof of God's faithfulness. You are a warrior, and warriors don't quit.

So when the next storm rises, don't bow down—lift your eyes and declare: "Look at God!"

Call to Action
Keep Walking With Me

Warrior, this isn't the end of our journey together—this is only the beginning. Thirty days may have passed, but your healing, your breakthrough, your next chapter is still unfolding. Don't stop here.

💜 STAY ENCOURAGED

If these devotionals spoke to you, imagine what God will do as you keep feeding your spirit. That's why I created The Wounded Warrior Podcast. It's raw. It's real. And it's full of conversations that meet you right where you are—whether you're crying in the car, sitting in the hospital, or just needing to know somebody else gets it. Subscribe on iHeartRadio, YouTube, and every major platform. Let's keep walking this thing out together.

STAY CONNECTED

I want to hear your story. Tell me how these 30 days shifted you. Drop me a note or connect at www.authorleshawn.com. You'll find my books, updates on events, and resources that keep the fire burning. Don't just read my journey—let me help you tell yours.

💼 SECURE YOUR FUTURE

Faith covers your soul, but wisdom covers your household. I know what it's like to lose, to worry, to wonder if everything will fall apart. That's why I'm passionate about legacy. As Here Is the Insurance Lady, I help families like yours protect what matters most—health, home, and hope. Visit www.hereistheinsurancelady.com and let's make sure your future is as covered as your faith.

MY HEART FOR YOU

You've walked with me for 30 days, and now I want to leave you with this: You are a warrior. Not because life has been easy, but because you're still standing when it tried to knock you down. Don't just close this book and move on—keep pressing, keep praying, keep preparing. And when life tries to take your breath, stop, lift your eyes, and declare with me: "Look at God!"

SCRIPTURE INDEX

SURRENDER & TRUST
- Romans 8:28 — Day 1
- Isaiah 41:10 — Day 2
- John 3:16 — Day 3
- Luke 15:20 — Day 4
- Luke 15:22–24 — Day 5

GRACE & FORGIVENESS
- Ephesians 2:8–9 — Day 6
- Ephesians 4:32 — Day 7
- 2 Corinthians 12:9 — Day 8
- Philippians 4:7 — Day 9
- Nehemiah 8:10 — Day 10

HEALING & RENEWAL
- Isaiah 40:31 — Day 11
- 2 Timothy 1:7 — Day 12
- Psalm 147:3 — Day 13
- 2 Corinthians 5:17 — Day 14
- Isaiah 40:8 — Day 15

Storms & Struggles

- Isaiah 43:2 — Day 16
- Psalm 107:14 — Day 17
- 2 Corinthians 12:9 — Day 18
- Galatians 6:2 — Day 19
- Revelation 12:11 — Day 20

Peace & Community

- Isaiah 26:3 — Day 21
- Proverbs 18:21 — Day 22
- 1 Thessalonians 5:11 — Day 23
- Joshua 1:9 — Day 24
- Romans 5:3–4 — Day 25

Testimony & Purpose

- Revelation 12:11 — Day 26
- Matthew 19:26 — Day 27
- 1 Chronicles 16:11 — Day 28
- Psalm 30:5 — Day 29
- Isaiah 64:8 — Day 30

Final Blessing Prayer

Father, I thank You for the warrior reading these words right now. Thank You for carrying them through 30 days of surrender, healing, and renewal. I speak peace over their mind, strength over their body, and fire in their spirit.

Lord, remind them daily that they are not forgotten, not abandoned, and not defeated. Cover their household, protect their family, and position them for every promise You've spoken.

And when the storms rise again, help them to lift their eyes, breathe deep, and say with confidence: "Look at God."

In Jesus' name, Amen.